1,000,000 Books

are available to read at

www.ForgottenBooks.com

Read online
Download PDF
Purchase in print

ISBN 978-0-428-11707-8
PIBN 11247667

This book is a reproduction of an important historical work. Forgotten Books uses
state-of-the-art technology to digitally reconstruct the work, preserving the original format
whilst repairing imperfections present in the aged copy. In rare cases, an imperfection in
the original, such as a blemish or missing page, may be replicated in our edition. We do,
however, repair the vast majority of imperfections successfully; any imperfections that
remain are intentionally left to preserve the state of such historical works.

Forgotten Books is a registered trademark of FB &c Ltd.
Copyright © 2018 FB &c Ltd.
FB &c Ltd, Dalton House, 60 Windsor Avenue, London, SW19 2RR.
Company number 08720141. Registered in England and Wales.

For support please visit www.forgottenbooks.com

1 MONTH OF FREE READING

at

www.ForgottenBooks.com

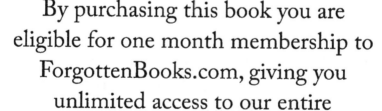

By purchasing this book you are eligible for one month membership to ForgottenBooks.com, giving you unlimited access to our entire collection of over 1,000,000 titles via our web site and mobile apps.

To claim your free month visit:
www.forgottenbooks.com/free1247667

* Offer is valid for 45 days from date of purchase. Terms and conditions apply.

English
Français
Deutsche
Italiano
Español
Português

www.forgottenbooks.com

Mythology Photography **Fiction**
Fishing Christianity **Art** Cooking
Essays Buddhism Freemasonry
Medicine **Biology** Music **Ancient**
Egypt Evolution Carpentry Physics
Dance Geology **Mathematics** Fitness
Shakespeare **Folklore** Yoga Marketing
Confidence Immortality Biographies
Poetry **Psychology** Witchcraft
Electronics Chemistry History **Law**
Accounting **Philosophy** Anthropology
Alchemy Drama Quantum Mechanics
Atheism Sexual Health **Ancient History**
Entrepreneurship Languages Sport
Paleontology Needlework Islam
Metaphysics Investment Archaeology
Parenting Statistics Criminology
Motivational

Historic, archived document

Do not assume content reflects current
scientific knowledge, policies, or practices.

BULLETIN OF THE
U.S. DEPARTMENT OF AGRICULTURE

No. 206

Contribution from the Bureau of Animal Industry, A. D. Melvin, Chief.
May 25, 1915.

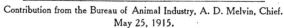

THE WOOLGROWER AND THE WOOL TRADE.

By F. R. MARSHALL and L. L. HELLER,
Of the Animal Husbandry Division.

CONTENTS.

	Page.		Page.
Introduction	1	Pounds of wool per pound of cloth	24
Present methods of disposing of wool by the growers	2	The need of improvement in handling American wools	24
Factors that determine the value of wool	3	How American methods of handling wool may be improved	27
Wool grading	11	Fundamental rules for the wool grower	29
Market grades	14	Glossary of terms used in the wool trade	31
Sorting wool	21		

INTRODUCTION.

The United States ranks as one of the principal wool-producing countries of the world. The amount of wool imported by American manufacturers is equal to more than one-half of the home-grown clip. American and foreign wools are often offered for sale at the same time in the warehouses of Boston and other wool-marketing centers. Some American wools are equally as valuable as the best foreign wools of the same class. On the whole, however, the appearance of American wools compares quite unfavorably with that of most of the foreign wools. The difference is due nearly altogether to the growers' methods of preparing the wool for shipment. Foreign woolgrowers, and Australians in particular, maintain a uniformly high standard in the handling of their wools. This care in preparation and the certainty as to the character of the contents of the bales has given their wools a high reputation that insures their bringing full value at the time of selling to the manufacturer.

Persons familiar with the buying and manufacturing of home-grown and foreign wools assert that on account of poor preparation

NOTE.—This bulletin discusses the preparation of wools for market and explains the effect upon the value of wool of the factors under the control of the grower. It is of interest to all sheep owners.

83237°—Bull. 206—15——1

BULLETIN 206, U. S. DEPARTMENT OF AGRICULTURE.

American wools net the grower from 1 to 3 cents a pound less than their actual value. This is due to the failure to classify the wool before selling and to defects from the use of improper twine, branding paints, and other minor causes.

The undesirable features which manufacturers have come to look for in American wools constitute a fixed charge which is borne by the producer. There seems to be little doubt that most of the work necessary to place American wools upon a parity with imported wools in our markets can best be done at the time of shearing.

Prevailing methods of selling do little to acquaint the grower with the manufacturers' complaints in regard to his output. In the range States where the clips are large the individual grower may establish for his wool a reputation that will enhance its selling price. To establish fully and realize the benefit of improved methods some form of cooperative effort is necessary. Especially is this true with farm wools where the single clip is small, and ordinarily passes through the hands of a number of uninformed dealers or local buyers and reaches the manufacturers only as part of an offering made up from a large number of clips, varying widely as to quality and care in preparation.

PRESENT METHODS OF DISPOSING OF WOOL BY THE GROWERS.

Western wools.—In the range States sheep are shorn either in sheds located on the premises of the sheep owner or at plants owned by individuals who employ shearers, fleece tiers, and sackers, and shear sheep from various owners at an agreed charge which includes all labor and material necessary to deliver the wool in sacks to its owner. Each individual owner attends to the selling of his own wool. In a few cases manufacturers send their buyers out to purchase wool direct from the growers, but the most of the clips are sold to buyers representing eastern dealers. There is no public market or wool exchange in this country. All transactions in the field or at the points where wool is concentrated by the dealers to be resold to manufacturers are made privately. The newspapers and trade and agricultural papers, upon which the grower must depend for information as to the value of his clip, base their reports of the wool market upon such facts as can be gathered from buyers or sellers at the main wool-selling centers, which are Boston, Philadelphia, Chicago, New York, and St. Louis. In some seasons wool is contracted for before shearing.

If unwilling to sell at the price offered at home the wool grower may consign his wool to a commission house and take chances upon the market falling or rising. Many concerns will either buy wool on speculation or accept it to be sold on commission. In neither case do the wool grower and the maufacturer come in contact with each other, and the former understands the defects of his wool and its handling only as there is chance opportunity to learn of them through the speculator or the distant commission agent.

During the past six seasons a growers' semicooperative selling agency has been in operation in Chicago, with branches in Boston and Philadelphia. The establishment has handled considerable wool, but according to report its growth and service have been less than might have been realized if growers had adhered to the policy of consigning their wool to it instead of using it as a lever to secure higher prices from buyers in the field.

Eastern wools.—The fact that much of the wool produced on farms of the Central and Eastern States is considered as secondary to mutton production does not lessen the need of giving the highest possible value to the grower. Here the producer is even farther removed from the manufacturer than in the case of the range sheepman, who can usually deal with some one acquainted with the values of wools and capable of distinguishing between clips varying in grade and quality. Considerable farm wool is sold to country storekeepers at a uniform price to accumulate into lots of sufficient size to be sold to a traveling buyer. In Minnesota and Wisconsin cooperative selling agencies have been established. The managers of these agencies put the entire amount received into suitable grades for selling to the manufacturers and set a fair price upon each lot of wool received.

Lack of contact between the manufacturer and the wool grower is largely responsible for the latter's failure to place his wool upon the market in such a way as to secure its full value. In order to dispose of wool to the best advantage growers must know the shrinkage and the proper class and grade names for their wools and be able to understand the reports of the market as published.

The pages that follow deal with the factors that determine the value of wool, market reports, grading, sorting, and methods of effecting improvement in the preparation of wool.

FACTORS THAT DETERMINE THE VALUE OF WOOL.

SHRINKAGE.

It is the buyer's first duty in inspecting an offering to make an estimate of the yield of clean or scoured wool. American wools may shrink from 25 to 80 per cent. Since more than 300 pounds of grease wool may be required to produce 100 pounds of scoured, the importance of shrinkage in the eyes of the buyer is readily recognized. Some of the wastes that occur during manufacturing can be used in other types of fabrics, but the loss in scouring is a complete loss.

Shrinkage is due first and chiefly to the oil present in varying quantities in all natural wool. The term "condition" has a special use in the wool trade, referring to the amount of oil or yolk and

4 BULLETIN 206, U. S. DEPARTMENT OF AGRICULTURE.

foreign matter and not to strength or color. Wool from sheep of the breeds that have been bred chiefly for fineness and weight of fleece carries much more oil than that from so-called coarse breeds, or those bred for mutton and having wool of relatively coarser fiber. The weight of a heavy, soggy, greasy fleece may gratify the grower, but the actual commercial value depends solely upon the amount and quality of the clean, scoured wool. American breeders as a rule consider that a large amount of oil is necessary and desirable in the production of a fine quality of wool. It is true that our best wools come from fleeces that shrink rather heavily from oil. At the same time much of the Australian wool shrinks very much less than that of the same fineness produced in this country.

Sand, dust, dirt, burs, and seeds also lower the yield as well as affect the value of the clean wool. The sand present is due to the storms that are experienced in some parts of the West. An instance is related of a sand storm making it necessary to suspend operation at a shearing corral for half an hour. At the end of that time the average weight of fleeces had risen from 6 to 9 pounds, which could hardly be attributed to growth of wool during that time. It is impossible to produce other than heavy-shrinking wools upon some of the sandy ranges, but if there is to be any profit from the operation the wools must be of good character otherwise.

In figuring shrinkages in this country there is no common standard. Some concerns scour cleaner than others, and scour different wools to varying degrees of cleanliness, according to the purpose for which they are to be used. Neither is there any standard as to the amount of moisture present after the wool has been dried. Hot tests are taken immediately after the wool is dried, while in the cold tests the wool has been allowed to "condition," or regain moisture for a time.

The dealers often have sample lots scoured for their own information, and the mills, before buying, may also make a test. Sometimes the shrinkage in the two tests will vary from 1 to 2 per cent, it being to the advantage of the mill to get out every vestige of grease in such a test. A good grader is supposed to estimate within 1 per cent of the actual shrinkage. It has been said that short-fibered wools shrink 2 to 3 per cent more than longer ones of similar character. This statement is in accord with what one would naturally suppose, but there are no available data to show this amount of difference.

Table 1 (prepared by the National Wool Warehouse and Storage Co., of Chicago) indicates the important part that shrinkage plays in fixing prices. At the top are the prices per pound of clean or scoured wool. These are applicable to wools worth from 40 to 70 cents, which limits will cover all ordinary cases. In the column to the left are the percentages of shrinkage. These run from 55 to 75. Take a case of clean wool being worth 40 cents. If it shrinks 60

THE WOOLGROWER AND THE WOOL TRADE.

per cent the wool is worth 16 cents in the grease. On the other hand, if the shrinkage is known and also the grease value, the clean value can be calculated readily.

TABLE 1.—*Relative prices of scoured and raw wool at varying percentages of shrinkage.*

Shrinkage. Per cent.	Price of clean or scoured wool (cents)—															
	40	41	42	43	44	45	46	47	48	49	50	51	52	53	54	55
56	18.0	18.4	18.9	19.3	19.8	20.2	20.7	21.1	21.6	22.0	22.5	22.9	23.4	23.8	24.3	24.7
57	17.6	18.0	18.5	18.9	19.4	19.8	20.2	20.7	21.1	21.6	22.0	22.4	22.9	23.3	23.8	24.2
58	17.2	17.6	18.1	18.5	18.9	19.3	19.8	20.2	20.6	21.1	21.5	21.9	22.4	22.8	23.2	23.7
59	16.8	17.2	17.6	18.1	18.5	18.9	19.3	19.7	20.2	20.6	21.0	21.4	21.8	22.3	22.7	23.1
59	16.4	16.8	17.2	17.6	18.0	18.4	18.9	19.3	19.7	20.1	20.5	20.9	21.3	21.7	22.1	22.6
60	16.0	16.4	16.8	17.2	17.6	18.0	18.4	18.8	19.2	19.6	20.0	20.4	20.8	21.2	21.6	22.0
61	15.6	16.0	16.4	16.8	17.2	17.5	17.9	18.3	18.7	19.1	19.5	19.9	20.3	20.7	21.1	21.5
62	15.2	15.6	16.0	16.3	16.7	17.1	17.5	17.9	18.2	18.6	19.0	19.4	19.8	20.1	20.5	20.9
63	14.8	15.2	15.5	15.9	16.3	16.6	17.0	17.4	17.8	18.1	18.5	18.9	19.2	19.6	20.0	20.3
64	14.4	14.8	15.1	15.5	15.8	16.2	16.6	16.9	17.3	17.6	18.0	18.4	18.7	19.1	19.4	19.8
65	14.0	14.3	14.7	15.1	15.4	15.7	16.1	16.4	16.8	17.1	17.5	17.9	18.2	18.6	18.9	19.3
66	13.6	13.9	14.3	14.6	15.0	15.3	15.6	16.0	16.3	16.7	17.0	17.3	17.7	18.0	18.3	18.7
67	13.2	13.5	13.9	14.2	14.5	14.8	15.2	15.5	15.8	16.2	16.5	16.8	17.2	17.5	17.8	18.2
68	12.8	13.1	13.4	13.7	14.1	14.4	14.7	15.0	15.4	15.7	16.0	16.3	16.6	17.0	17.3	17.6
69	12.4	12.7	13.0	13.3	13.6	13.9	14.3	14.6	14.9	15.2	15.5	15.8	16.1	16.4	16.7	17.1
70	12.0	12.3	12.6	12.9	13.2	13.5	13.8	14.1	14.4	14.7	15.0	15.3	15.6	15.9	16.2	16.5
71	11.6	11.9	12.2	12.5	12.8	13.0	13.3	13.6	13.9	14.2	14.5	14.8	15.1	15.4	15.7	16.0
72	11.2	11.5	11.8	12.0	12.2	12.6	12.9	13.1	13.4	13.7	14.0	14.3	14.6	14.8	15.1	15.4
73	10.8	11.0	11.3	11.6	11.9	12.1	12.4	12.7	13.0	13.2	13.5	13.8	14.0	14.3	14.6	14.9
74	10.4	10.6	10.9	11.2	11.4	11.7	11.9	12.2	12.5	12.7	13.0	13.3	13.5	13.8	14.0	14.3
75	10.0	10.2	10.5	10.7	11.0	11.2	11.5	11.8	12.0	12.2	12.5	12.8	13.0	13.2	13.5	13.8

Shrinkage. Per ct.	Price of clean or scoured wool (cents)—														
	56	57	58	59	60	61	62	63	64	65	66	67	68	69	70
55	25.2	25.6	26.1	26.5	27.0	27.4	27.9	28.3	28.8	29.2	29.7	30.1	30.6	31.0	31.5
56	24.6	25.1	25.5	26.0	26.4	26.8	27.3	27.7	28.2	28.6	29.0	29.4	30.0	30.4	30.8
57	24.1	24.5	24.9	25.4	25.8	26.2	26.7	27.1	27.5	28.0	28.4	28.8	29.2	29.7	30.1
58	23.5	23.9	24.4	24.8	25.2	25.6	26.0	26.5	26.9	27.3	27.7	28.1	28.6	29.0	29.4
59	23.0	23.4	23.8	24.2	24.6	25.0	25.4	25.8	26.2	26.7	27.1	27.5	27.9	28.3	28.7
60	22.4	22.8	23.2	23.6	24.0	24.4	24.8	25.2	25.6	26.0	26.4	26.8	27.2	27.6	28.0
61	21.8	22.2	22.6	23.0	23.4	23.8	24.2	24.6	25.0	25.4	25.7	26.1	26.5	26.9	27.3
62	21.3	21.7	22.0	22.4	22.8	23.2	23.6	23.9	24.3	24.7	25.1	25.5	25.8	26.2	26.6
63	20.7	21.1	21.5	21.8	22.2	22.6	22.9	23.3	23.7	24.0	24.4	24.8	25.2	25.5	25.9
64	20.2	20.5	20.9	21.2	21.6	22.0	22.3	22.7	23.0	23.4	23.8	24.1	24.5	24.8	25.2
65	19.6	20.0	20.3	20.7	21.0	21.4	21.7	22.1	22.4	22.8	23.1	23.5	23.8	24.2	24.5
66	19.0	19.4	19.7	20.1	20.4	20.7	21.1	21.4	21.8	22.1	22.4	22.8	23.1	23.5	23.8
67	18.5	18.8	19.1	19.5	19.8	20.1	20.5	20.8	21.1	21.5	21.8	22.1	22.4	22.8	23.1
68	17.9	18.2	18.6	18.9	19.2	19.5	19.8	20.2	20.5	20.8	21.1	21.4	21.8	22.1	22.4
69	17.4	17.7	18.0	18.3	18.6	18.9	19.2	19.5	19.8	20.2	20.5	20.8	21.1	21.4	21.7
70	16.8	17.1	17.4	17.7	18.0	18.3	18.6	18.9	19.2	19.5	19.8	20.1	20.4	20.7	21.0
71	16.2	16.5	16.8	17.1	17.4	17.7	18.0	18.3	18.6	18.9	19.1	19.4	19.7	20.0	20.3
72	15.7	16.0	16.2	16.5	16.8	17.1	17.4	17.6	17.9	18.2	18.5	18.8	19.0	19.3	19.6
73	15.1	15.4	15.7	15.9	16.2	16.5	16.7	17.0	17.3	17.6	17.8	18.1	18.4	18.6	18.9
74	14.6	14.8	15.1	15.3	15.6	15.9	16.1	16.4	16.6	16.9	17.2	17.4	17.7	17.9	18.2
75	14.0	14.3	14.5	14.8	15.0	15.3	15.5	15.8	16.0	16.3	16.5	16.8	17.0	17.3	17.5

CLASSES OF WOOL.

The value of wool is influenced more or less by its length and it is classified accordingly. The longer wools are known as "combing" and the shorter ones as "clothing." These classes are shown in Plate I. This classification is founded upon the English or Bradford system of manufacture, which requires a wool to be about 2½ inches long to be successfully combed. The lower grades of combing wools are usually considerably longer than this, as the coarser wool generally

BULLETIN 206, U. S. DEPARTMENT OF AGRICULTURE.

has more length. Clothing wools are shorter. Of late years a class
midway between the two has sprung up, known as "baby combing."
The French combs handle this length of staple quite satisfactorily.

The combing wools are used in worsted manufacturing. Only the
longer straightened fibers are used and these are placed parallel in
the yarn. The short, broken, and tangled fibers are removed and
make up the "noils." Not only is length required, but also strength.
Tender wools will not stand the combing process and are unfitted
for this purpose, regardless of length. None but virgin [1] wools are
used in the manufacture of worsteds.

Clothing wools are used in the manufacture of woolens, felts, etc.
The fibers are laid in every direction, and instead of attempting to
arrange them parallel as in worsteds, the opposite extreme is desired.
Noils, shoddy, etc., can be used in this process of manufacture.

The difference in value between combing and clothing wools is
from 2 to 6 cents per scoured pound in favor of the former.

Coarse, low wools more or less resembling hair are classed as
carpet wools. A very small amount of these are produced in America,
most of those used being imported from Asia. Some Navajo wool
is used in carpet manufacture.

The factors that determine the length of the wool are not all under
the control of the flockmaster. The wool does not grow so long on
old sheep as it does on a young animal, but short pasture and faulty
methods of herding tend to decrease the normal length. Some sheep
have been bred for longer staple and naturally produce a greater
length of fiber than others

GRADE.

Wool is graded according to fineness, and generally the finer the
grade the better the price per scoured pound. Because of their low-
shrinking qualities, coarser wools in the grease may sell for as much
as or more than the finer ones, but when cleaned there may be as
much difference as 20 cents a pound in price. The various grades
are discussed on pages 14 to 21.

CHARACTER IN WOOL.

Character in wool will scarcely admit of definition, yet it is very
important. Sometimes this may only be acknowledged by prefer-
ence, or a greater demand at the same price, but at other times
there is a difference in price. Color would come under this heading.
A white wool is often desired rather than one of a creamy tinge,
as the latter tint often shows up after scouring. A wool with lots
of "life" or "nature," which means that the fibers are sound and
lustrous and that the yolk is of a uniform consistency rather than
clotted, is desirable. "Lofty" is another word used to describe a

[1] See glossary of wool terms at end of bulletin for explanation of technical words and phrases.

THE WOOLGROWER AND THE WOOL TRADE.

superior wool of considerable crimp that is uniform in character. Lofty wools possess considerable elasticity and spin higher than those lacking this quality. In well-grown wools the staples or locks are more distinct and the fibers are more nearly parallel than in the frowzy wools. Fleeces from poorly bred sheep show greater variation in diameter of fiber and are more likely to "run out" on the flanks, and this wool is consequently not so valuable. Black fiber shows up occasionally among mutton-bred sheep, and it is objectionable. Kempy wool is worth several cents a pound less than a similar quality free from this defect which denotes poor breeding.

TENDER WOOL.

Wool that has a weak part somewhere in its length must generally go into the clothing class, and in some instances it is inferior even for this. The exact cause of "tender" wool is not always known. It is generally agreed that sickness, a sudden shock from a blizzard, lack of feed, a rapid change from green to dry feed, or vice versa, and overfeeding often cause this condition. Sickness will often cause a distinct "break" in the fiber throughout the fleece. In general, better care and housing conditions decrease the percentage of tender wool, yet this is not always the case. Sheep that have been largely allowed to rough it, but having plenty of feed, have been known to produce better clips than the flock closely housed. "Frowziness" often indicates tender wool. After the wool has been clipped it may become tender through becoming wet. Tender wools are worth several cents per scoured pound less than sound wools. Plates II and III show well-grown, tender, and frowzy wools.

USE OF PAINT FOR BRANDING.

The practice of branding the sheep with paint is very generally established throughout the range country. The brands are usually placed upon the shoulders, side, or back—the most valuable parts of the fleece. Under some conditions it is doubtless necessary to brand, but tar brands should be avoided and the brands used should be as small as possible. At the present time most of the American dealers recognize no brand as soluble in scouring, but regard all paint locks with distrust. The damage done by the paint can scarcely be estimated. It is not only the damage to the locks directly affected, but the fibers carrying the paint are more or less mixed throughout the fleece, and it is almost impossible to get them all out. The amount of damage done varies with the kind of wool and the use to which it is put. One of the prominent felt manufacturing concerns that uses large amounts of the Texas wools for fine felts tries by every means to eliminate the paint. The painted wool is separated in

8   BULLETIN 206, U. S. DEPARTMENT OF AGRICULTURE.

sorting, and yet the scoured wool contains so many specks that it is necessary to "hand pick" it. This process costs from 3 to 5 cents per scoured pound, and with the quantities handled by this firm in one year the expense amounts to between $8,000 and $10,000. This concern will pay one-half to 1 cent extra for wool suitable to its need guaranteed free from paint. Another manufacturer writes: "If the brand marks on a lot of wool were unfailingly and altogether soluble it would enhance its value to us about one-fifth of a cent per pound, the usual cost of clipping." It is good practice to clip off the brands before shearing.

TAGS.

Tags are worth about one-third as much as good wool, depending somewhat upon condition. Ordinary tags shrink much more in scouring than the fleece proper taken from the same sheep. Most clips have the tags on the inside of the fleeces. In buying wool containing tags the buyer usually discounts enough so that he will be safe. It is generally better to remove the tags so that the exact amount can be ascertained, as the grower will generally fare better under this system. It must be admitted, however, that the custom of discounting 1 per cent for tags even after they have been sacked separately does not recognize the value of separate sacking. Another very serious objection to allowing tags to remain in the fleece is that they are likely to stain the surrounding wool, especially when it is wet.

WET WOOL.

Wet wool has been known to "take fire," and there are numerous instances where it has been damaged to the extent of from 1 to 2 cents per pound. The damage is not altogether due to the weakening of the fiber, but also to staining, especially when there are any tags present.

Often wool must be hauled for long distances and piled up along the tracks waiting for shipment. In such case it is sometimes subjected to heavy rain, and while the bags apparently dry out where the air has access, there is no chance for drying inside the pile. When the bags once become wet it often takes months for them to dry out. It is said that as much as 10 per cent of the wools from one of the western States was damaged by moisture in 1913.

WOOL CONTAINING BURS.

Burry fleeces should be separated from the others if there are very many burs present. The hard burs can usually be knocked out during the process of manufacture with a little extra work, but the soft burs entail considerable extra expense. They often open up in a spiral or

Bul. 206, U. S. Dept. of Agriculture. PLATE I.

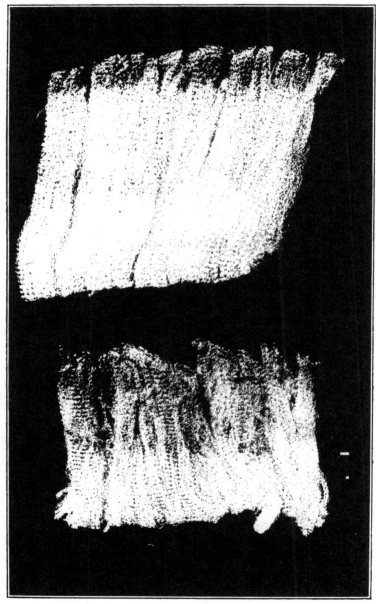

COMBING (UPPER) AND CLOTHING (LOWER) WOOLS.

Bul. 206, U. S. Dept. of Agriculture.   PLATE II.

WELL-GROWN WOOL.

Bul. 206, U. S. Dept. of Agriculture. PLATE III.

FIG. 1.—FROWZY WOOL.

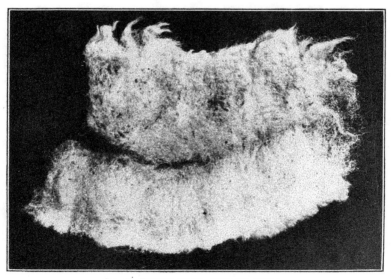

FIG. 2.—TENDER WOOL, SHOWING BREAK.

Bul. 206, U. S. Dept. of Agriculture. PLATE IV.

Wool Packed in Old Sacks and Poorly Sewed.

corkscrew shape and can not be separated in carding. Such wools may be run through a bur picker, which, together with the bur guards on the card, removes them. In the shorter extremely burry wools the process of carbonizing is practiced. This consists of treating with sulphuric acid or aluminum chlorid and heating to about 200° F. The burs and vegetable matter are charred and then removed by crushing and dusting. The process costs from 1½ to 3 cents a pound and results in an average loss of about 10 per cent in weight. Often the shrinkage due to burs is much more than this. Combing wools that are extremely burry are rarely if ever carbonized, as this injures the wool to a certain extent, even under the most favorable circumstances.

IMPROPER TYING OF FLEECES.

The evil of tying the fleeces with sisal twine is constantly recurring. Volumes have been written against this curse of the wool trade, but it is continually coming up again, although of late years it has not been so uniformly common. The "fleece" or farm wools are worse in this respect that the "Territory." A discrimination in price of from 1 to 5 cents a pound and the refusal of some dealers to handle wool thus put up have not eliminated this practice. The pieces of sisal twine adhere to the wool through the processes of manufacture and seriously injure the finished fabric. The large rough jute twine is also undesirable because of the fibers coming off in the fleeces. Growers should insist on having the fleeces in compact bundles that will not open in the ordinary processes of packing.

Locks.—Locks are loose pieces of wool that fall out when the fleeces are handled. They may represent some of the best qualities of the wool, but because of their being in small pieces they are difficult to sort, hence the buyers object to them when they are present in large quantities. Their presence can be avoided by proper tying.

PACKING THE BUCK FLEECES.

Probably the average sheepman can see no reason for keeping the bucks' fleeces separate; nevertheless there is one. These fleeces, especially among the fine and medium wooled sheep, are considerably heavier in grease, and it is undesirable to have too great a variation in shrinkage among fleeces of one grade. The buck fleeces are as a rule easy to detect; they are large, have a strong, musky odor, and the yolk of the fleece has a greenish cast. The statement has been made that the spinning qualities of bucks' fleeces are also lower, but there are no good grounds for this contention. A discount of 50 per cent is often charged against the buck fleeces in western selling contracts. Discrimination to this extent is seldom warranted for buck fleeces sold in the grease.

BLACK WOOL.

No other of the "off sorts" do more damage by being packed with the other wool than the black fleeces. After wool has been packed in bags for a time the fleeces "freeze" together more or less; that is, locks from one fleece adhere to neighboring ones. A lock of black wool in any wool intended for white goods is capable of doing untold damage. To be sure, not all wool goes into white goods, but the dealer, when he is having the wool graded, often does not know to whom it will be sold, nor for what purposes it will be used. The only way to be safe is to pick off all the black locks from the adjacent fleeces. Black wool has been in demand for making a natural gray in the past, but at the present time it is not especially sought after and it sells at from 1 to 2 cents a pound less than the corresponding grade of white wool. When shearing takes place the blacks should be cut out and sheared by themselves, and their wool packed separately and so labeled.

COTTED OR MATTED FLEECES.

The badly cotted or matted fleeces should be placed separately, because it is necessary to run them through an opener, which is not done with ordinary wool. This necessarily causes the breakage of fibers to increase. There are really two kinds of cotts, hard and soft. A soft cott, if it is not in too bad condition, may go through with the other wool.

EFFECTS OF DIPPING.

The effects of dipping upon wools are not always the same. In the Southwest, where there is considerable sand and dirt in the fleeces, it tends to lighten them, while in the Northwest it is said that dipping increases the weight. Most of the dips that have been used do not have any very harmful effect upon the wool, but dealers and manufacturers claim that lime-and-sulphur and caustic-soda dips are harmful. However, no tests have been made in America upon the spinning qualities of dipped and undipped wools.

HAND AND MACHINE SHEARING.

The practice of hand shearing is still quite common in parts of the West. Ridges of wool are left over the sheep's body, and the short wool of the head and belly is largely left on the sheep. Much of the wool is shorter than it would be if machine shorn, and a considerable portion of it is double cut. The large amount of short and cut fibers results in a greater percentage of noil in the combing wools and reduces their value accordingly. Many wools grade as clothing instead of combing solely because of being hand shorn.

In some sections where rapid changes of weather are experienced, the sheepmen object to machine shearing on the ground that the sheep will blister during hot weather if shorn too closely. Losses

THE WOOLGROWER AND THE WOOL TRADE. 11

duo to a cold wavo following close shearing have also bccn reported. However, machine shearing does not necessarily mean close shearing, as thicker combs can be used and the fiber cut at a greater distance from tho skin; but it docs insure more uniformity. A great deal of tho prejudice against machine shearing has been aroused by improper handling of the machines.

PACKING WOOL.

Packing lamb, ewe, and wether fleeces together militates against higher prices for wool. Lambs' wool is usually more valuable because of lighter shrinking qualities and because of the fact that it will spin higher than wool from older sheep. Sewing the bags with sisal or other unsuitable twine also creates a bad impression in the mind of the buyer, as there is always the possibility of the sisal fiber getting into the wool and causing damage. Much wool is lost through the bursting of the bags. This is caused by the use of poor twine. A stronger twine used for sewing, such as Andover six-ply, is recommended for this purpose. Examples of poor packing are shown in Plate IV.

Packing dead wool (wool from dead sheep) with good wool is also far too common. The dead wool is usually worth about half as much as the corresponding grade of good wool. Another feature in bad packing that should be discouraged is the tying of the fleeces together. In many cases the two fleeces are not of the same grade and they must be separated by the grader before being assigned to any pile.

Occasionally one hears of frauds being practiced by putting stones, etc., in the center of a fleece or sprinkling sand over the wool after it is shorn, but the actual cases of this kind are very rare. It is true that foreign materials have been found in wool sacks, varying from spectacles to oil stones, but such occurrences are more often due to accident than to intent to defraud.

WOOL GRADING.

Most American-grown wool is sacked just as the fleeces come from the sheep and sold at home to dealers. Before offering wool to the manufacturer the dealer makes up from his various purchases a number of piles, each containing only fleeces of similar character and value. This work constitutes grading and should not be confused with the sorting done at the mill. In the dealer's warehouse the fleeces are not untied, but are graded on the basis of judgment of the fleece as a whole. (Plate V.)

The grading itself is an art with which few American sheepmen are familiar, yet it has many points of interest for them. Passing through the lofts and merely seeing the fleeces go over the grading

12 BULLETIN 206, U. S. DEPARTMENT OF AGRICULTURE.

board is not enough to give one an insight into the complexity of a trade that requires at least three years' apprenticeship. Days and even weeks must be spent there before the importance and significance of numerous points that arise can be appreciated.

The grade has much to do with fixing the price of wool, and every woolgrower should be competent to know how his own wool will grade in the market. The various grades are described later on in connection with the market report following the outline of the work of the grader. Some clips of finer wools, very uniform in character, are resold to the manufacturer in the original bags. This is practicable when the mill produces a variety of fabrics for which different grades of wool are required. (Plate VI.)

AT THE GRADING TABLE.

About the grading table or board are a number of large baskets or box trucks, one for each grade. The wool sacks are rolled up by the table, the ends and one side ripped or cut down, depending upon the kind of sewing, and the fleeces turned out in a roll. The fleeces are separated by helpers, who throw them upon the table. Other helpers bring up the bags and empty the baskets containing the graded fleeces, piling them ceiling high where the wool can be examined by the prospective buyers.

The different grades are merely arbitrary divisions more or less clearly recognized and defined in trade. There is some variation from year to year and among the different houses. The mills often have a higher standard of qualities than the dealers, and the "half-blood" of the dealer may represent the millman's idea of a "three-eighths blood." Fineness is the dominant factor; but many other things are considered in grading.

The grader does not determine fineness, as might be supposed by examination of individual fibers. The handling of innumerable fleeces has given him an intuitive sense of quality, so that he accomplishes in an instant what would take an untrained person a much longer time. For example, say that a half-blood combing fleece has been thrown upon the board. This grade has in general certain characteristics, such as a certain degree of crimp (the finer the crimp the finer the wool, except in very fine wool), and a certain arrangement of the fibers in locks or staples that the grader notes as soon as his eye rests upon it. This gives him something as a guide, but the grade is not yet decided. When his hands come in contact with the fleece he has another source of information. The feel of the different grades is more or less characteristic, and this sense is highly developed in the grader. Illustrating this, a blind buyer formerly operated upon the market with considerable success. He could not only make purchases and distinguish the grade by the touch, but by the odor he

THE WOOLGROWER AND THE WOOL TRADE. 13

could also tell the section of the country from which some wools came. Finer wools usually shrink more than coarser wools, and too wide a range of shrinkage is not desired in any grade, as the scouring liquor is made up of a strength suitable for the average shrink of the grade; thus a higher shrinking fleece would not be suitably scoured.

The grader knows also that a half-blood fleece usually shrinks around 60 per cent, depending upon the season and the location where grown. If the fleece in question is heavier-shrinking, say 65 per cent, the grader will probably take a second look to be sure that he has not "lost his eye." If his first impression as to fineness was correct and the fleece is typically half-blood, or perhaps a trifle high, it will probably be thrown a grade higher, that is, fine medium, on account of its heavy shrinking qualities. The next fleece might offer another problem. Say this one is what is known as a "line" fleece. It is midway between the three-eighths-blood and the quarter-blood. It can go either way. The chances are that if the three-eighths-blood wool has been sold and the dealer is well satisfied with the sale, this fleece will find a resting place on the three-eighths-blood pile. Other conditions might decree it to be a quarter-blood. If the market demands for three-eighths-blood wool were high and the supply a trifle short there would also be some "crowding" of the grades and the three-eighths-blood as a whole would probably average a little lower. There are also "line" fleeces midway between combing and clothing. These are sometimes made into a separate grade known as French combing. It is thus seen that the grades manifest more or less elasticity, depending upon market conditions.

Another fleece might be puzzling because of the wool of the "britch" being much coarser than that of the shoulder. For example, the shoulders might be half-blood quality or higher, while the "britch" was quarter-blood. The grader would simply use his best judgment and trust to chance that the fleece would remain as he throws it. At best the grades can only contain fleeces which contain a large proportion of the quality of wool represented by the grade names. Graded wool ready for sale is shown in Plate V, figure 2.

14 BULLETIN 206, U. S. DEPARTMENT OF AGRICULTURE.

MARKET GRADES.

The following is a copy of a common form of market report as published in trade and agricultural papers in November, 1914:

BOSTON WOOL MARKET.

Domestic Wools.

OHIO AND PENNSYLVANIA FLEECES.

Delaine washed	28	@ 29
XX	27	@ 28
Fine unmerchantable	25	@ ..
½-blood combing	28	@ 29
⅜-blood combing	28	@ 29
¼-blood combing	26½	@ 27½
½, ⅜, ¼ clothing	23	@ ..
Delaine unwashed	23	@ 24
Fine unwashed	23	@ 24
Common and braid	23	@ 24

MICHIGAN AND NEW YORK FLEECES.

Fine unwashed	23	@ ..
Delaine unwashed	21½	@ 22
½-blood unwashed	27	@ 28
⅜-blood unwashed	27	@ 28
¼-blood unwashed	26	@ 27
½, ⅜, ¼ clothing	21	@ 22
Common and braid	23	@ 24

WISCONSIN AND MISSOURI.

⅜-blood	26	@ 27
¼-blood	26	@ 26½
Braid	22	@ 23
Black, burry, seedy cotts	18	@ 19
Georgia	22	@ ..

KENTUCKY AND SIMILAR.

½-blood unwashed	28	@ ..
⅜-blood unwashed	...	@ 28
¼-blood unwashed	27	@ ..
Common and Braid	23	@ 24

BOSTON WOOL MARKET—Contd.

Scoured Basis.

TEXAS.

Fine 12-months	56	@ 58
Fine 8-months	53	@ 54
Fine Fall	45	@ 47

CALIFORNIA.

Northern	54	@ 55
Middle County	51	@ 52
Southern	48	@ 50
Fall free	46	@ 48
Fall defective	38	@ 40

OREGON.

Eastern No. 1 staple	60	@ ..
Eastern clothing	57	@ 58
Valley No. 1	48	@ 50
Valley No. 2	44	@ 45
Valley No. 3	39	@ 40

TERRITORY.

Fine staple	60	@ 62
Fine medium staple	58	@ 60
Fine clothing	57	@ 58
Fine medium clothing	55	@ 57
½-blood combing	59	@ 60
⅜-blood combing	49	@ 51
¼-blood combing	53	@ 54

DOMESTIC WOOLS.

Ohio and Pennsylvania.—In the foregoing report, which is typical for American wools, the Ohio and Pennsylvania fleeces head the list. These really include the West Virginia clip also. The fine wools from these States are the strongest in the world and they are the most valuable of American wools. More than half of the flocks are of Merino breeding. The sheep pasture upon well-covered sod land and the wools contain little sand or dirt. The entire shrinkage is therefore due to the natural grease. A complete classification of these wools is as follows:

COMBING WOOLS.	CLOTHING WOOLS.
Delaine.	XX and X, washed or fine unwashed.
Half-blood.	Half-blood clothing.
Three-eighths-blood.	Three-eighths-blood clothing.
Quarter-blood.	Quarter-blood clothing.
Low quarter-blood.	
Braid.	

All of the above grades are not always given in the market report. Sometimes not all of them are to be found upon the market and they are eliminated.

Many years ago there were two higher grades, Picklock and XXX, representing, respectively, the wool of the Silesian Merino and the American and Silesian Merino cross. These grades are no longer used upon the market, but they are occasionally seen in some of the mills making very fine woolens. More often these qualities occur only as sorts representing parts of fleeces. The amount of this wool produced, however, is very small and is still diminishing.

The XX grade represents the fineness or quality of an ideal American Merino. Delaine wools are combing wools of this and of X quality. Sometimes they are quoted Fine Delaine, being X quality and above, and Medium Delaine, being about half blood in quality. They are not necessarily from the Delaine type of Merino. The X quality is supposedly the wool from a sheep containing three-quarters Merino blood. It is sometimes referred to as three-quarters blood. Market usage has decreed that XX and X as grade names shall be used only in referring to washed clothing wools, but the terms are sometimes used to indicate the same degrees of quality in other wools. Fine unwashed contains these same qualities, but these wools are heavier shrinking.

Half-blood, three-eighths-blood, and quarter-blood grades, as the terms were coined, referred supposedly to wools from sheep of half, three-eighths, and quarter Merino blood, but they have no such significance now. Wools grading as high as half blood can come from sheep having no trace of Merino blood; the purebred Southdown, for instance, produces wool that sometimes grades that high, and this breed has been kept pure from outside blood for centuries. On the other hand, quarter-blood would rarely come from a sheep containing any Merino blood. Low quarter blood is a grade lower than quarter blood, and braid is the lowest grade of all. It usually refers to luster wool, such as might come from a Lincoln or a Cotswold sheep.

Washed wools.—The practice of washing the sheep has given rise to the terms of washed, unmerchantable, and unwashed. The unmerchantable wool is not unsalable wool, but that which has been poorly washed—sometimes the sheep are merely "driven through the

16   BULLETIN 206, U. S. DEPARTMENT OF AGRICULTURE.

creek." Such fleeces shrink more than those properly washed and could not be fairly placed in an offering of washed wool, as their loss in scouring would be much greater. Fleeces may be unmerchantable for other reasons. These terms do not always mean that the washing operation has actually taken place, the practice of washing being on the decline, but sometimes refer solely to shrinkage. The washed wools are lighter in color and condition, shrinking 3 or 4 per cent less than the unmerchantable, and the latter shrinks about the same amount less than the unwashed.

Michigan and New York.—Michigan and New York have the same classification and the wools are quite similar, some of them being fully as good as Ohio and Pennsylvania wools. As a whole, however, they are not quite up to this standard. The wools from the above States are quite frequently spoken of as the "fleece," "domestic," "native," or "farm" wools.

Kentucky and similar.—Kentucky, Indiana, Missouri, and Wisconsin wools are not so fine in character. They rarely grade higher than half or three-eighths blood, as most of the sheep are of the mutton type. The pasture is much the same as in the "fleece" wool States. The term "bright" is sometimes applied to the wools of these States.

Parts of Tennessee and Virginia are given over to the spring-lamb industry and they produce some wools of a medium quality. Much of it is consumed by local knitting mills. This is some of the lightest shrinking wool in America, some of it not going higher than 35 per cent. Georgia and some of the other Southern States produce some rather coarse, light-shrinking wools.

SCOURED BASIS.

Texas.—Wool from Texas and the "territories" is usually quoted on a scoured basis. The reason for this is that there is such a wide variation in shrinkage in different localities and also from season to season that the clean basis is more satisfactory. In Texas shearing twice a year is often practiced. These short wools are probably the best American felting wools. They are also highly regarded in certain branches of woolen manufacture. The 12-months clip of Texas is probably as near the Ohio type of wool as any western wool. The Merino blood is still strongly dominant here. These wools sometimes shrink as low as 56 to 58 per cent. The average for the entire State, however, has been estimated at 66 per cent. The spring and fall Texas wools come to market untied.

California.—The California wools are quoted as northern, middle, and southern counties. The northern counties wool usually represents a year's growth, and is the most valuable. In the middle and southern counties the wool shrinks more, and shearing is often prac-

Fig. 1.—Grading Wool at Warehouse.

Fig. 2.—Graded Wool Ready for Sale.

Bul. 206, U. S. Dept. of Agriculture. PLATE VI.

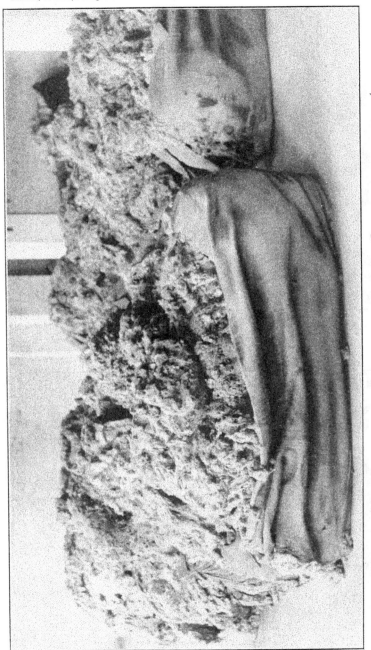

AMERICAN WOOL ON DISPLAY IN THE ORIGINAL BAG.

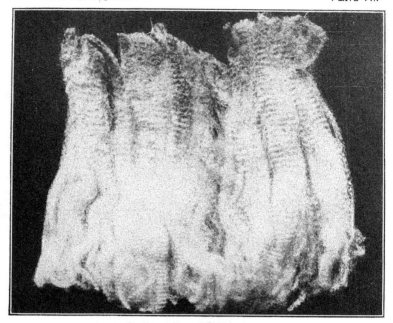

Fig. 1.—Combing or Staple Wool of "Fine" Grade.

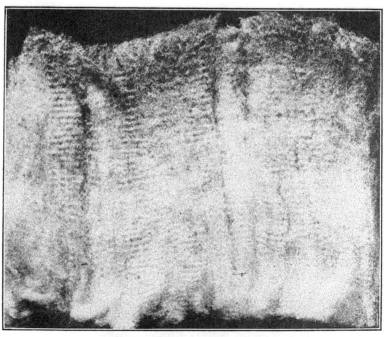

Fig. 2.—Half-Blood Combing Wool.

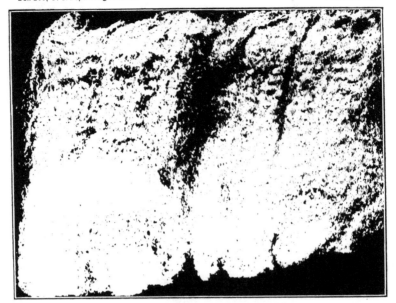

Fig. 1.—Three-Eighths-Blood Combing Wool.

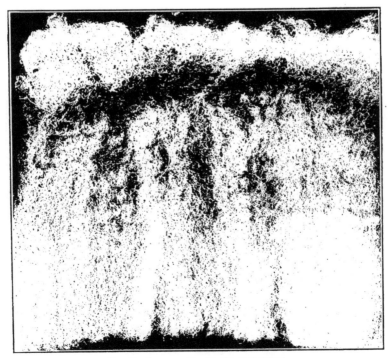

Fig. 2.—Quarter-Blood Combing Wool.

THE WOOLGROWER AND THE WOOL TRADE. 17

ticed twice a year. There are spring, or 8 months, and fall, or 6 months, wools from these sections. The spring wool is usually longer and it shrinks less than the fall. Both spring and fall wools are highly regarded for felting purposes. This is due to the fact that they contain a high percentage of Merino blood and also to the fact that they are short. In the southern part of the State the mestiza bur is very common and many of the wools contain it in varying quantities. These wools are quoted as "defective" in distinguishing them from the "free" wools. This bur can not be removed by mechanical means; hence the wools must be carbonized. The short wools are not tied up in fleeces, but come to market in a loose condition. Some of the California wools are baled to facilitate shipping.

Oregon wools.—Oregon produces some excellent wool, though it is somewhat high in shrinkage. The best of it will grade 80 per cent of staple or combing wool. Excepting the valley wool, it is largely of a fine and fine-medium character. The Lakeview wools of this State are sometimes spoken of separately. The valley wools are quite different from the ordinary clip. They are largely from long-wooled sheep. They are quoted as valley No. 1, No. 2, and No. 3, corresponding roughly to half-blood, three-eighths-blood, and quarter-blood, respectively. These numbers have this same general significance when applied to wools from other sections. The valley wools are somewhat akin to the luster wools of England. Some buyers claim that the heavy rainfall of the valley discolors the wool to a certain extent, but others deny this. These wools are the only western wools that lose weight under normal conditions when being shipped east. They lose from 1 to 2 per cent. Most other wools if dry when shipped gain this amount or even more in transportation.

TERRITORY WOOLS.

Under "territory wools" are grouped all those wools produced west of the Missouri River, and they derived their name from the fact that this section of the country was formerly made up of Territories in distinction to the States of the central and eastern sections. Certain of the wools, however, have more or less distinct characteristics which separate them from the main lot, and they are no longer included in the territory wools. Among these are the clips of California, Oregon, Texas, Arizona, and New Mexico.

The States that produce the territory wools—Montana, Wyoming, Idaho, Utah, Nevada, Colorado, and Washington—are in the main the range States. A great deal of fine-wool blood is present in the flocks, but the use of medium and long wool mutton rams is steadily increasing, and this is having its effect upon the character of wool produced. Considerable sections of the range are more or less sandy

18 BULLETIN 206, U. S. DEPARTMENT OF AGRICULTURE.

and the grass is not as thick as in the central and eastern part of the country. The wind blows with considerable force, creating sand storms in some sections, and much sand and dirt are deposited upon the sheep. These conditions give rise to a heavy-shrinking wool, as would naturally be expected. The wools containing sand usually shrink more than those containing mountain dirt. Occasional fleeces from this district shrink more than 80 per cent, and the average for the different States ranges from 63 to 70 per cent. There is often considerable variation in shrinkage from year to year in the wools from any particular locality. When there has been snow on the ground during the winter, the clips are often 5 per cent lighter than when the range is bare. The selling of territory wools upon the market is consequently upon a clean or scoured basis.

Classification and grades of territory wools.

COMBING.

Fine staple
Fine medium staple. } usually one grade.
Half-blood staple.
Three-eighths-blood staple.
Quarter-blood staple.
Low quarter-blood staple.
Coarse, common, low, or } often one grade.
  braid.

CLOTHING.

Fine clothing.
Fine medium clothing. } usually one grade.
Half-blood clothing.
Three-eighths-blood clothing.
Quarter-blood clothing, or short quarter-
  blood.

Practically all three-eighths-blood and quarter-blood wools are of combing length.

The term "staple" as applied to a territory wool refers to a combing wool. "Ordinary" is sometimes used to designate clothing wool in this section instead of referring to quality. The terms of fine, fine medium, medium, and low medium have arisen and are used in a general way in referring to territory wools. They are often used in referring to original lots and are largely equivalent to the following:

Fine   =XX and X qualities, or fine staple and fine clothing.
Fine medium=X, half-blood and three-eighths-blood.
Medium   =Three-eighths-blood and quarter-blood.
Low medium=Low quarter-blood and braid.

It is rather difficult to attempt to characterize the wools from each State, as they grade almost imperceptibly into one another. Often differences appear in the wools that can be recognized, but are difficult to describe.

Montana.—Montana wools as a whole are probably the best of the territory clips. They are light-shrinking compared to the wools of the neighboring States, of good length, and attractive in appearance. They have a slightly creamy tinge which shows up even after scouring. Their felting qualities are good. It is sometimes claimed that wools from this State are more likely to be tender than some of the others, but if this is true the other grade qualities, such as length and quality, overbalance it.

Wyoming.—Wyoming wool has not the soft characteristic feel of the Montana wools. It is somewhat "wild" or harsh in nature. This is said to be due to the influence of the alkali soil over which many of the sheep pass. Wyoming wool scours out very white. It is quite strong, robust, and of fair length, but is a heavy-shrinking wool. The shrinkage varies widely from year to year. Because of its scouring out so white some manufacturers prefer it to Montana when its heavier shrinkage is discounted.

Idaho.—The Triangle or Soda Springs wools come from a section around the town of the latter name in Idaho. The three points of the triangle are Ogden, Utah; Pocatello, Idaho; and Granger, Wyo. The wools from this section are somewhat lighter-shrinking than the surrounding ones.

The wools from western Idaho are long and fine (often grading 80 per cent staple), but in the eastern part of the State they are generally somewhat shorter.

Utah, Nevada, Colorado, and Washington.—Much of the Utah wool is rather short, there being little staple in it. Overstocking the range is said to be responsible to a certain extent for the poorer qualities of the wools from this State. Nevada is a high-shrinking wool of fairly good quality.

Colorado wool has little character, being a nondescript wool often shrinking from 70 to 72 per cent. There are, however, some lighter-shrinking wools (around 60 per cent) of good quality from certain sections of the northern part of the State. The wool from this State in general is often described as being "breedless." It rarely grades higher than one-half-blood. In southern Colorado the sheep are sometimes sheared twice a year, this short wool coming to market untied.

Washington as a whole probably produces the heaviest-shrinking wools of any western State. It is estimated that the average shrinkage is around 70 per cent. This high shrinkage is due to natural grease, of which there is a great deal in the wool of this section, and to dirt, etc., in the fleeces.

New Mexico and Arizona.—New Mexico and Arizona wools are very uneven in character. The care given the flocks is often very slight, while many of the sheep are poorly bred, and the fleeces run out and kempy. The wools are often very poorly put up. The shrinkage varies from 40 to 75 per cent, though dipping often lightens the wool from these States. It is said that wool from flocks owned by Americans, on account of better handling, is worth an average of 2 cents a pound more than that from flocks of Mexican owners. The

20   BULLETIN 206, U. S. DEPARTMENT OF AGRICULTURE.

Navajo wool is very uneven. It comes to market untied, the low quarter-blood mixed with the fine grade.

Dakotas, Kansas, and Nebraska.—The wool from the Dakotas, western Kansas, and Nebraska are sometimes included in the territory wools. They are really midway between the "bright" and the territory in condition, having more sand and dirt than the bright but not as much as the territory. The term "semibrights" is sometimes applied to them.

Terms used in other market reports.—The reports of the St. Louis markets often refer to the shrinking qualities of the wool as light-fine, heavy-fine, etc. The amount of vegetable matter present is also indicated by burred, slightly burred, etc. Some other terms are also used that are usually self-explanatory.

FOREIGN GRADES.

Basis of foreign classification.—The quality of English and many other foreign wools is often designated by the counts or number of hanks per pound. The coarser wools are represented by the lower counts, as 18's, 24's, 36's, etc., and the finer ones as 64's, 70's, 80's, etc. These numbers or counts represent the hanks per pound of top to which the wool is supposedly capable of being spun, each hank representing 560 yards. Thus, wool of 50's quality should spin 50×560 yards per pound of top, if spun to the limit. This classification is based on the worsted system of manufacture.

TABLE 2.—*Foreign wool classes and corresponding counts for American grade.*

American grades.	Foreign classes— top-maker's quality.	Counts often spun to in America.
Fine	60's–70's	50's–60's
Half-blood	56's–60's	40's
Three-eighths blood	50's–56's	36's
Quarter-blood	46's–50's	32's
Low quarter-blood	40's–46's	20's
Low, coarse, common, or braid	36's–40's	16's

As a matter of fact the top-maker's quality does not actually represent the counts to which the wool can be spun. The lower grades will not spin up to their number, while the finer ones will spin much higher than their designated numbers. Some fine American wools have been spun to 200 counts for exhibition purposes. Short wools will not spin as high as similar wools of greater length, hence this factor also influences the counts to which the wool will spin.

Another fact worthy of mention is that the wools are rarely spun to their limit, that is, to as fine a yarn as is possible to spin. Wool can be spun several counts higher in England than it can in America. This is due to the fact that the air is moister there and that the labor of the

THE WOOLGROWER AND THE WOOL TRADE. 21

mills is more capable than in the United States. This does not imply that American fabrics are inferior to imported, as a better cloth results if the wool is not so highly spun.

GRADES OF WOOL FROM VARIOUS BREEDS OF SHEEP.

It is impossible to assign wool to a particular grade solely upon the basis of the breeding of the sheep. In the mutton breeds especially there are wide variations within a single breed and within flocks. The following list shows in a general way how wool from the various breeds would be likely to grade:.

BREED.	GRADE OF WOOL PRODUCED.
Merino (eastern States)	Delaine, XX, X, or fine unwashed, etc.
Merino (range States)	Fine and fine medium staple or clothing.
Rambouillet	Fine and fine medium staple or clothing and a small amount of half-blood.
Southdown	Half and three-eighths blood (chiefly three-eighths combing or clothing, chiefly clothing).
Shropshire	Mainly three-eighths-blood, combing or clothing. Some quarter-blood.
Hampshire	Three-eighths and quarter blood combing or clothing.
Dorset	Three-eighths and quarter blood combing or clothing.
Suffolk	Three-eighths-blood combing and clothing.
Cheviot	Quarter-blood combing.
Oxford	Quarter and low quarter-blood combing.
Corriedale	Three-eighths-blood combing.
Cotswold	
Lincoln	Low quarter-blood combing or braid.
Leicester	
Crossbred: Long wool on Merino or Rambouillet	Half-blood, three-eighths-blood, and quarter-blood combing.
Crossbred: Shropshire or Hampshire on Merino or Rambouillet.	Half-blood and three-eighths-blood combing or clothing.

SORTING WOOL.

While wool is graded at the warehouses, as a rule sorting is done only at the mills. Its object is to secure lots of wool having greater uniformity as to fineness than could possibly be obtained if the fleeces were not divided. The wool as it grows upon the sheep's body varies in length and quality; consequently the fleeces can not be uniform in quality throughout. There is usually a wider range of quality in the coarse wools, such as Lincolns and Cotswolds and the crossbreds, than among the fine wools. Coarser fleeces might be of a three-eighths-blood grade or even half-blood on the shoulder, while the "britch" would be a quarter-blood. The shoulder wool is considered the best for strength, quality, and length, the sides

BULLETIN 206, U. S. DEPARTMENT OF AGRICULTURE.

are next best, and the quality decreases passing backward until the "britch" is reached, which is the coarsest part of all. The wool from the back is likely to contain hayseed or chaff, and it is not of as good quality or strength as that from the shoulder. It is also often shorter. The belly wool is usually finer than any, but it is short, "frowzy," is not so strong, and it lacks character. The wool from over the head is short, coarse, and in the black-faced breeds is likely to contain black fibers. Modern machinery could probably handle these different qualities of wool in the same lot, but more uniform yarn can be made and the wool spun to a finer thread if it is sorted, hence it is an economical advantage to do the sorting. The work is not as exacting as it once was; as a rule not as many sorts are made now as formerly.

The sorting is done over a table that has either a slatted or wire-mesh top, so that the dirt will fall through. The fleeces are untied, shaken out, and piled up beside the table and then passed over the board. A good light is necessary to do the work properly.

The number of sorts made from a fleece or from a bag of wool and the quantity of each will naturally vary with the quality of the wool, the mill where the sorting is done, and the goods for which the wool is intended. Ordinarily four to five major sorts would take care of the bulk of the wool, along with as many more off sorts. There is no uniform system of designating the sorts; each mill uses its own names or numbers.

The regular sorts are made mainly upon quality and length. A little extra length will sometimes cause wool to be thrown higher because of resulting higher spinning qualities. Often the best of a sort, the longer wool, will be separated and used for warp, as a stronger yarn is needed for this purpose than for filling. · The off sorts are usually something out of the ordinary. In a worsted mill they are sold for other purposes, as they can not be manufactured on the worsted system.

RESULTS OF SORTING A SAMPLE BAG OF WOOL.

The percentage of the various sorts may vary considerably. The proportion of the main sort varies from 50 to 80 per cent of the weight of a lot of fleeces of a common grade. This is because the quality, condition, and length of the different wools vary, and the dealers' and millmen's ideas concerning grades are not always the same. The market conditions and the quality of the goods into which the wool is to be made may also influence the sorting.

The following is the record of an actual case of sorting a bag of wool, showing the weight, percentage, and value per pound of each sort. This bag contained fleeces that had been graded in the ware-

THE WOOLGROWER AND THE WOOL TRADE. 23

house as "half-blood." The gross weight, was 245 pounds; weight of bag, 4¼ pounds; net weight of wool, 240¾ pounds.

TABLE 3.—*Results of sorting a bag of half-blood Montana wool.*

Sort.	Weight.	Percentage.	Value per pound.
Regular sorts:	*Pounds.*	*Per cent.*	*Cents.*
X or three-quarters-blood	11.21	4.66	21.0
Half-blood combing	88.69	36.84	22.7
Half-blood clothing	12.90	5.36	21.6
Three-eighths-blood combing	64.76	26.90	23.0
Three-eighths-blood clothing	24.33	10.11	20.0
Quarter-blood combing	12.90	5.36	19.0
Short quarter-blood	4.55	1.89	17.0
Low quarter-blood	.55	.23	16.0
Off sorts:			
Stained and gray	.55	.23	14.0
Shorts	3.90	1.62	10.0
Fribs	3.32	1.38	5.0
Clips	2.76	1.15	1.0
String	1.37	.57	....
Loss in sorting	8.90	3.70	....

DESCRIPTION OF SORTS.

Little need be said concerning the regular sorts. They merely represent a more complete division according to quality than was possible in grading. Regarding the off sorts, the "stained and gray" sort is not usually made, except when white goods are to be manufactured and it is necessary to separate them out of the main lot. Their character is implied by their name.

Shorts consist of short wool such as grows about the face and eyes. Part of it may also be due to double cutting in shearing. Fribs are short, sweaty, and dungy locks. Clips are locks so incrusted with foreign material that the wool can not be freed in scouring, but must be clipped off. The string cut from the fleeces is practically valueless, since considerable paper twine is used. The loss of weight in sorting depends upon whether the wools contain much sand or dirt. Other off sorts are often made from wools of various sections. Tags are a very common one. They are sometimes separated at shearing time, but quite often they are separated by the sorters. They are large dung locks and are worth less than half of the value of the other wool.

Paint locks are another quite common sort. The free wool is clipped from the paint, and the short fiber containing paint is sold to hat manufacturers, etc. It is worth about 1½ to 2 cents a pound.

Seedy wool is a sort containing weed seeds, soft burs, etc., that will not be removed by the manufacturing process. It must often be carbonized before using. These carbonized wools are used largely for woolens, felts, etc.

About 25 per cent of the wool bags can be used again; the rest are sold and bring from 5 to 10 cents a pound.

POUNDS OF WOOL PER POUND OF CLOTH.

Some printed statements convey the impression that the entire fleece goes into the production of a garment, so that the amount of finished cloth is equal to the amount of scoured wool. This impression is erroneous, not only because of a certain amount of wool of other sorts than the main ones being present, but also because there is more or less loss all the way along the process of manufacture. True, these other sorts are of value, but they are not generally worth nearly as much as the main lot.

As the weight per yard of goods varies, it is not feasible to give the amount of wool required to manufacture a garment, suit, or so many yards of cloth, but the pounds of wool per pound of cloth can be given. A number of tests reported by different mills and published in the bulletin of the National Association of Wool Manufacturers show that for woolen goods from 3 pounds to 4.64 pounds of grease wool, with an average of 3.73 pounds, were required to make 1 pound of cloth. The average amount of scoured wool required was 1.37 pounds. For worsted cloths from 2.56 pounds to 4.55 pounds of grease wool was required, with an average of 3.66 pounds. The average amount of scoured wool for 1 pound of worsted cloth was 1.55 pounds.

THE NEED OF IMPROVEMENT IN HANDLING AMERICAN WOOLS.

From the discussion in the foregoing pages it can readily be seen that dealers and manufacturers confront many difficulties in handling the average clip of American wool.

PRESENT CONDITIONS.

In October, 1913, the Animal Husbandry Division of the Bureau of Animal Industry, in cooperation with the Bureau of Crop Estimates, made a canvass of a number of sheep owners in Western States to determine the extent to which growers follow the best practices. Because of the way in which the names were secured it is probable that the 383 replies received were from men whose methods are superior to those generally followed in the same localities; consequently the percentages shown at the foot of the table are much higher than would be reported if it had been possible to receive replies from all wool growers in the States shown. The results of this canvass are shown in Table 4.

Bul. 205, U. S. Dept. of Agriculture.   PLATE IX.

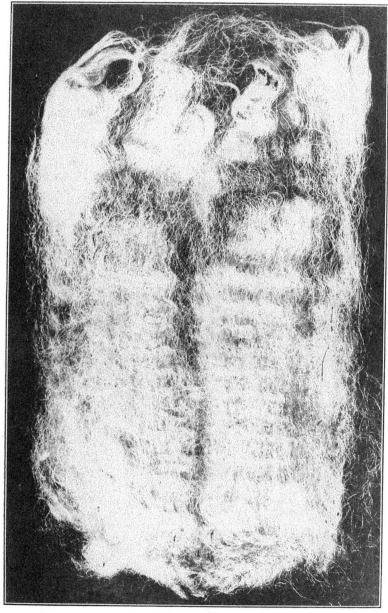

LOW QUARTER-BLOOD COMBING WOOL.

Bul. 206, U. S. Dept. of Agriculture. PLATE X.

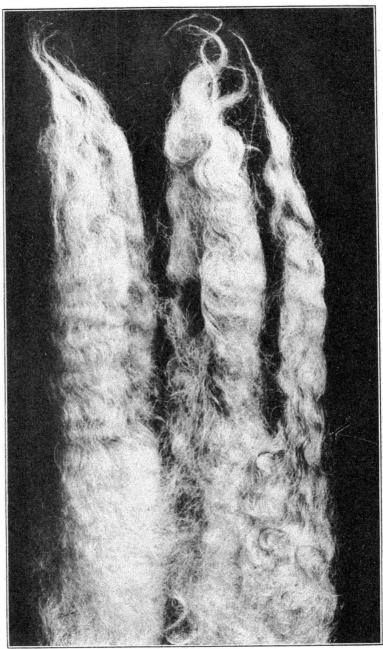

BRAID WOOL.

Bul. 206, U. S. Dept. of Agriculture. PLATE XI.

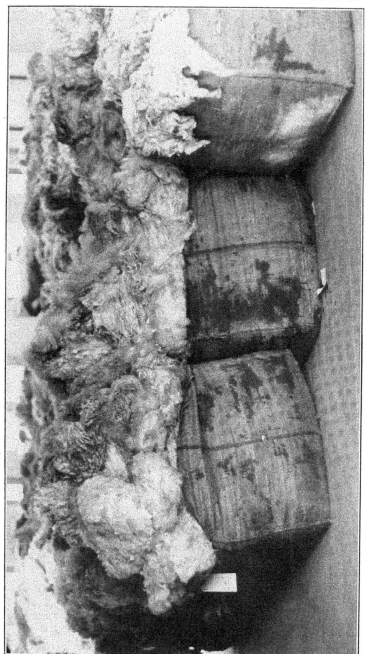

Foreign Wool Skirted, Classed, and Baled, on Display at Boston.

THE WOOLGROWER AND THE WOOL TRADE.

TABLE 4.—*Results of investigation of methods of western sheepmen in marketing wool.*

State.	Number of sheep shorn in 1913 by persons reporting.	Number of persons reporting.	Number who sacked ewe, lamb, and buck wool separately.	Number who sacked blacks separately.	Number who used paper twine.	Number who sacked tags separately.	Number of cases where dockage was made for tags.
Arizona	134,422	18	9	6	2	9	3
California	125,302	26	10	5	8	4	7
Colorado	109,695	13	6	8	8	3	4
Idaho	336,249	62	32	48	49	45	26
Montana	518,049	82	46	28	44	51	37
New Mexico	92,011	13	6	10	3	5	....
Oregon	195,246	37	25	23	34	26	11
Utah	309,583	71	17	58	61	24	36
Washington	77,419	13	7	....	11	3	4
Wyoming	371,029	48	32	40	39	33	13
Total	2,269,005	383	190	226	259	203	141
Per cent of total	....	....	49.3	59.0	67.6	53.0	....

Practically one-half the correspondents separated ewes', lambs', and bucks' wool when sacking; 59 per cent put up the black wool separately; and 53 per cent sacked the tags separately. It must be borne in mind, as stated before, that these percentages are undoubtedly much higher than would be the case if it were possible to secure replies from all woolgrowers in any section or State.

The American wool clip is sold by the growers unclassified and in the main very poorly handled. The way in which each of the various defects injures the manufacturing value of the wool has been explained in previous pages. These defects have come to constitute a fixed charge against American wool, which does not apply to wools coming to this country from Australia and some other countries.

Probably the lack of any form of classifying or grading before selling causes the greatest loss to our woolgrowers. The buyer, whether he represents a mill or a firm that buys wool to be sold again after grading, is expected to place a fair valuation upon clips in which there may be many sacks each containing three or four grades of wool. The difference in the scoured values of those grades may not be so serious, but the difference in shrinkage, say, between quarter-blood and half-blood fleeces, is a very great one, and there is no possibility of doing more than making an estimate of the average shrinkage and value of the clip as it is offered. Manifestly the buyer must place the shrinkage estimate sufficiently high to protect himself from loss. In order to get a certain quantity of a particular grade he must buy, even of graded wools, a lot containing other grades that must be sold after sorting.

26 BULLETIN 206, U. S. DEPARTMENT OF AGRICULTURE.

MANUFACTURER'S TEST OF FOREIGN AND DOMESTIC WOOL.

Even after grading in the eastern warehouses American wools often sell below foreign wools of similar grade and quality because the latter have been skirted and carefully classified before baling, while American fleeces go to the mills in the same shape as they leave the shearing floor, being graded so far as is possible without untying the fleeces.

Comparative results from two lots of wool, one American (Idaho Soda Springs) and one foreign (Australian 50's crossbred), of the same grade and the same value on a scoured basis, as given by a Philadelphia manufacturer, are shown below:

TABLE 5.—*Sorting and scouring test of domestic and foreign wool.*

Item.	Soda Springs.	50's crossbred.
Cost in grease..cents..	18.5	28.0
Loss in weight...per cent..	1.96	.87
Shorts, strings, clips, low, etc...................................do....	11.25	.17
Main sorts..do....	86.79	98.96
Actual shrinkage main sorts from total weight of wool purchased..............do....	57.89	37.36
Shrinkage of net weight of wool scoured...........................do....	51.46	36.70
Actual cost main sorts in grease..................................cents..	20.06	28.29
Cost per clean pound...do....	41.32	44.69

As is shown by these figures, the manufacturer bought the American wool for 3.37 cents per clean pound less than exactly similar foreign wool. This was possible mainly because the former lot contained only 86.79 per cent of what was really wanted, against 98.96 per cent in the case of the foreign wool that had been skirted and put up without string. The amount and value of the off sorts in American wools varies, and to the extent of that variation the purchase of these wools involves uncertainty that partakes of gambling and necessitates buying at a figure low enough to cover loss in use or sale of the part not wanted and the greater expense of sorting.

It is the grower who eventually pays all penalties and suffers most of the loss due to inferior preparation of wool. It must not be overlooked that the Australian sheep raiser incurs considerable expense in his method of preparing his wool for the market. He enjoys some advantages favoring the production of extra quality, most marked in the case of fine wools. In the case above cited the wools were of the same grade and the comparison is wholly fair, as the net result shown is on the scoured basis and for wools of equal clean value.

METHODS OF BUYING AND SELLING.

It is the time-honored and oft-repeated statement that buyers pay little attention to the individual clip. Instances are cited in which the dealer buys clips without having seen the wool. However, the dealer may know more concerning the clip than the grower is aware of. He knows the amount of shrinkage for the section for a number of

THE WOOLGROWER AND THE WOOL TRADE. 27

years previous. He knows of the weather conditions, whether or not the winter has been an open one, and he estimates the shrinkage accordingly. He knows whether or not there has been a blizzard and if the wool is likely to be tender. He knows something of the breeding of the sheep and how the owner runs them, for these are all matters of knowledge throughout the country. In fact, he has many sources of information that act as a general guide to values. Yet the grower very often receives little or no benefit for extra pains taken in growing and preparing the wool, and he has just grounds for complaint. In this connection he must appreciate the fact that comparatively few clips are large enough to yield the amount of wool of any one grade that is called for at one time by a manufacturing concern. This being the case, the "fine staple" or the "half blood" of one clip has to be thrown with that of one or more other clips to form a commercial parcel. Unless the buyer of the individual clips is positive that each one has been put up in the same good way he can not insist upon receiving a greater price from the millmen, because they will not relax their safeguards while there is danger of even a very small amount of damage from paint, poor twine, or any one of the vexatious causes that experience has shown are to be looked for.

HOW AMERICAN METHODS OF HANDLING WOOL MAY BE IMPROVED.

If some plan can be worked out whereby American wools can be prepared for market in a manner similar to foreign wools, while they are still the property of the growers, it should be to the advantage of all concerned.

GRADING ON THE RANGE.

It has been claimed that on account of the American growers' comparative nearness to market he should make no attempt to grade his clip. How sound this claim is depends upon how cheaply and how well the work can be done on the range. There is no question that the wool is in better condition for grading immediately after shearing than at any later time. Grading without baling has been practiced in several instances in the west, but the only resulting advantage has been to enable the owner to determine more nearly the value of his clip.

BALING ON THE RANGE.

The statement has been made that baling western wools would militate against higher prices because of resulting poorer appearance. Some southern Wyoming wools have been baled ungraded for a number of years, and a dealer who handles a considerable portion of these says they have not been damaged. Possibly if this wool was baled to the density of foreign wool without being graded and the tags removed, injury would result. The reason these wools have been baled is because they received the benefit of a more favorable freight rate.

Ordinarily the sheep owner can not know as much about the demands of the market and how the wool should be graded as does the wool grader, or, as he is called in Australia, the "classer." This man must always work to the same standard. Attempts of various owners by whom he might be employed to make his work conform to their own ideas would render impossible that uniformity in the classer's work which is necessary to hold the confidence of the buyer as to the put up of the clips.

SKIRTING THE FLEECES.

Skirting fleeces consists in the removal of the belly and the other less valuable parts. When wools are skirted the belly is separated

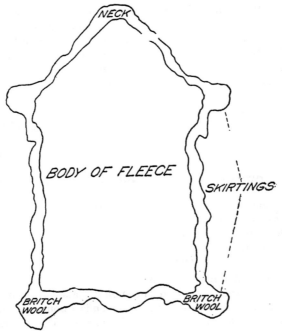

FIG. 1.—Diagram showing portion of fleece ordinarily removed in skirting.

by the shearer and skirting consists of the removal of the parts indicated in figure 1. The belly wool has already been removed from the fleece shown in this figure. The advantage of this lies in the fact that some manufacturers needing higher qualities of wool can buy the bodies of the fleeces alone when they would not care to incur the trouble and expense of separating and reselling the inferior parts, as is necessary when entire fleeces are purchased.

MARKETING GRADED AND SKIRTED WOOL.

The grading and skirting of western American wools is not likely to be economical or satisfactory where less than 10,000 to 20,000 sheep are shorn at one plant. This number need not be the property of one individual, but the wool from such a number should be put up by the same standard and that standard should be the same as applies in other plants in the same territory if our wools are to be as highly esteemed in the markets as foreign wools of the same scoured value.

It is wholly desirable and practicable that small sheep owners, where suitably located, should combine to erect and use a common shearing plant to be conducted upon a high standard. If the practice of grading and skirting is to be adopted some provisions other than those now prevalent will be necessary. The skirtings, locks, and tags from each flock will have varying values, while the main part of the clip will contain not less than two or three grades varying too widely for use by a single mill. An individual wool seller would, therefore, have even greater need than at present of being posted regarding wools and the markets. He would also need to have connection with various branches of the trade in order to dispose of each of the various lots of wool into which his clip was divided. In case of cooperation in ownership and management of the shearing plant the same organization might also be used in effecting the sale of the wool, or each grower might sell at home as opportunity offered or consign to the establishment appearing likely to give the best service.

Marketing farm wools.—For farm wools the greatest advantage is likely to come through such cooperation as will insure the grower's receiving the value of his wool after grading and sale along with other clips sufficient in amount to allow of selling in lots containing not less than 4,000 or 5,000 pounds of each grade.

FUNDAMENTAL RULES FOR THE WOOL GROWER.

Until further improvement can be wrought there are a number of rules that no grower on either farm or range can afford to neglect in order to enhance the reputation of his clip and also—what is equally necessary—the reputation of the wool of his section. These are:

1. Adhere to a settled policy of breeding the type of sheep suitable to the locality.
2. Sack lambs', ewes', wethers', and all buck or very oily fleeces separately. If the bucks or part of the ewes or wethers have wool of widely different kind from the remainder of the flock, shear such separately and put the wool in separate sacks so marked.
3. Shear all black sheep at one time, preferably last, and put the wool in separate sacks.

30   BULLETIN 206, U. S. DEPARTMENT OF AGRICULTURE.

4. Remove and sack separately all tags, and then allow no tag discount upon the clip as a whole.

5. Have slatted floors in the holding pens.

6. Use a smooth, light, and hard glazed (preferably paper) twine.

7. Securely knot the string on each fleece.

8. Turn sacks wrong side out and shake well before filling.

9. Keep wool dry at all times.

10. Make the brands on the sheep as small as possible and avoid tar brands.

11. Know the grade and value of your wool and price it accordingly.

12. Do not sweat sheep excessively before shearing.

13. Keep the floor sweepings out of the wool.

14. Do not sell the wool before it is grown.

15. When all these rules are followed place your personal brand or your name upon the bags or bales.

GLOSSARY OF TERMS USED IN THE WOOL TRADE.

Black wool.—Includes any wool that is not white.

Braid wool.—Grade name, and synonym for luster wools.

Britch wool.—Wool from the lower thighs of the sheep; usually the coarsest on the body.

Carbonized wool.—That which has been treated with a solution of aluminum chlorid or sulphuric acid to remove the vegetable matter. Carbonizing is rarely practiced with worsted wools.

Carding.—Consists of opening the wool staples, separating to a certain extent the fibers, and condensing and delivering the opened wool in a continuous strand or sliver.

Carpet wool.—Low, coarse wool used in the manufacture of carpets. There is very little produced in the United States.

Combing.—An operation in worsted manufacture which straightens the fibers and separates the short, weak, and tangled fibers known as noils from the continuous strand of long parallel fibers known as top.

Come-back.—In America this refers to a wool fine in quality and having more length than would ordinarily be expected. In Australia it is the result of breeding crossbreds back toward pure Merinos, one of the parents being a pure Merino.

Condition.—Refers to the degree of oil in grease wool. It largely regulates the price. In scoured wool it is used to indicate the degree of moisture.

Cotted fleeces.—A cotted fleece is one in which the fibers are matted or tangled. The cause may be ill health of the sheep or the absence of the proper amounts of yolk or grease in the wool.

Cow tail.—A very coarse fleece, more like hair than wool.

Crimp.—The natural waviness of wool fiber. Uniformity of crimp indicates superior wool.

Crossbred wools.—In the United States the term generally refers to wool from a longwool and finewool cross.

Defective.—Denotes that something will show disadvantageously after the wool is scoured. Fire, water, or moths may cause defective wools. California burry wool is quoted as defective.

Delaine wool.—Delaine originally referred to a fine type of women's dress goods. Delaine wools are fine combing or worsted wools, from Ohio and vicinity, but not necessarily from the Delaine Merino.

Fall wool.—Wool shorn in the fall where shearing is practiced twice a year, as in California and Texas. The fall wool is usually dirtier than the spring clip. It represents from four to six months' growth.

Filling (weft).—Threads that run crosswise and fill in between the warp.

Fribs.—Short and dirty locks of small size. Dungy bits of wool.

Frowzy wool.—A lifeless appearing wool with the fibers lying more or less topsy-turvy. The opposite of lofty wool.

Grease wool.—Wool as it comes from the sheep with the grease still in it.

Hogget wool.—English term for the first wool from a sheep.

Kemp.—Not a dead hair, but an abnormal fiber made up entirely of horny material, such as is on the outside of ordinary wool fiber. It will not dye as well as the ordinary fiber and does not possess spinning qualities.

Line fleeces.—Those midway between two grades as to quality or length.

Lofty wool.—Open wool, full of "life." Springs back into normal position after being crushed in the hand.

Luster wool.—That from Lincoln, Leicester, and Cotswold sheep. It is known as luster wool because the coarse fibers reflect the light.

32 BULLETIN 206, U. S. DEPARTMENT OF AGRICULTURE.

Modock.—Wool from range sheep that have been fed and sheared in the farm States. The wool has qualities of both regions.

Noil.—A by-product of worsted manufacture consisting of short and tangled fibers. It is used in the manufacture of woolens.

Off sorts.—The by-products of sorting. In fine staple or any other grade there are certain quantities of short, coarse, stained, and colored wools. These are the off sorts.

Picklock wool.—Formerly a grade above XXX. Picklock was the product of Silesian Merino blood. There is no American market grade of that name at present; a little of this quality of wool is produced in West Virginia.

Pulled wool.—Wool taken from the skin of a slaughtered sheep's pelt by slipping, sweating, or the use of depilatory.

Quality.—The diameter of the wool. It largely determines the spinning quality.

Run-out fleece.—One that is not uniform but much coarser on the "britch" than elsewhere. It may be kempy.

Shafty wool.—Wool of good length and spinning qualities.

Shearlings.—Short wool pulled from skins of sheep shorn before slaughtering. Also English term for yearling sheep.

Shivy wool.—A somewhat broad term. It refers to the presence of vegetable matter in the wool.

Shoddy.—Wool that has been previously used for manufacturing purposes, torn apart and made ready to use again.

Skirting.—Skirting fleeces consists in removing the pieces and the low-quality wool of the britch from the edge of the fleece.

Spring wool.—Six to eight months' growth; shorn in the spring where sheep are shorn twice a year.

Stained wool.—That which is discolored by urine, dung, etc.

Staple.—(*a*) A lock or bunch of wool as it exists in the fleece. (*b*) Western combing wool.

Stubble shearing.—Shearing some distance from the skin, leaving a "stubble."

Suint.—Excretions from sweat glands deposited in the wool.

Sweating sheds.—Sheds in which sheep are "sweated" before shearing. The purpose is to raise the yolk and make shearing easier.

Tags.—Large dungy locks.

Territory wools.—Territory wools are in general those that come from the territory west of the Missouri River.

Tippy wool.—Wool in which the tip or weather end of the fiber is more or less incrusted.

Top.—A continuous untwisted strand of the longer wool fibers straightened by combing. After drawing and spinning it becomes worsted yarn.

Top-maker's qualities or counts.—Top-maker's qualities or counts are the numbers used in designating the quality of certain foreign wools. They range from 12's upward. The numbers are supposed to indicate the number of hanks of yarn a pound of top will spin to. Each hank represents 560 yards.

Tub washed.—Wool that has been washed after having been sheared. Very rare in America; was formerly practiced in Kentucky.

Virgin wool.—Wool that has not previously been used in manufacturing.

Warp.—The threads that run lengthwise in cloth.

Washed wools.—Those from which the suint has been removed by washing the sheep before shearing.

Wether.—In English wools it refers to wool other than the first clip from the sheep. In sheep, a castrated male.

Yolk.—The fatty grease deposited upon the wool fibers from the oil glands.